Pinkston Preparatory Collegiate Academy

School Planner

Created by Tracey K. Hurst
Cover by Thomas D. Hurst

Learn more about Early College High School
echsguidebook.com

Learn more about P-Tech
ptech.org

All rights reserved. No part of this publication may be reproduced, distributed, or transmitted in any form or by any means, including photocopying, recording, or other electronic or mechanical methods, without the prior written permission of the author, except in the case of brief quotations embodied in critical reviews and certain other noncommercial uses permitted by copyright law. For permission requests, write to the author at echsguidebook@gmail.com with, "Attention: Permissions - Guide Book," in the subject line.

Copyright © 2019 Hurst Educational Services
All rights reserved.
ISBN: 9781699721506

Table of Contents

Important Information to Remember	4
DISD Help Lines	5
DCCCD Help Lines	5
Distinguished Level of Achievement	6
My College Plan	7
What is it about reading?	8
Common Instructional Framework	9
Classroom Talk Starters	10
Generic WTL prompts	10
Collaborative Group Work Roles	11
Multiplication Table/Perfect Squares	12
Costa's Levels of Inquiry	13
Atlas	109
Reading Tracker	113
Test Tracker	115
Gemetrix Tracker	117
Classroom Lessons with Microsoft Programs Tracker	119
Dual Credit Program Monitoring	120
Missing Assignment Tracker	121
Math Formulas & More	124
Planner Check	126
Calendar	128

Important information to Remember

At any Dallas ISD location: DELL/HP log on to computer.
Username: (7-digit student id#) _____   Password: _____

Dallas ISD email – Outlook   www.outlook.com/dallasisd   Password: _____
7-digit ID (only):

Forgot password → www.password.dallasisd.org – must have completed *6 Challenge Questions*
If you are locked out and/or cannot sign in, provide your birthday.

Chromebook/Google Drive
Username: 7-digit id# @dallasisd.org   Password: _____

Google Classroom   https://classroom.google.com/u/0/h

Clever   http://clever.com/in/dallasisd   Log in with Google

All In Learning   https://plus.allinlearning.com/user/login/home

Edmentum   https://ple.platoweb.com/Account/Signin   Acct login: _____

Microsoft Tutorials - Gmetrix Console 8 Username: First.Lastname Password: _____

Edmodo   edmodo.com   Log in with DISD Google Drive Information

Keyboarding   typing.com   Username: 7 digit id#   Password: Touch2018

EverFi   https://platform.everfi.net
Register → Registration Code → Enter student information →
Username: First.Lastname Password: _____

EConnect → https://econnect.dcccd.edu/   ECampus https://ecampus.dcccd.edu/
DCCCD ID# _____

El Centro Email   http://outlook.dcccd.edu/   e1234567@student.dcccd.edu

Free Dart GoPass: https://www.dcccd.edu/services/onlineservices/discounts/pages/dartgopass.aspx

DISD HELP LINES

Dallas ISD Fraud Hotline   800-530-1608
This bilingual and confidential hotline is available 7 days per week and you can remain anonymous. This hotline is intended to report criminal, unethical, and other inappropriate behaviors within the Dallas Independent School District.

Dallas ISD Safe Schools Hotline: 214-932-5622
This hotline is to report crimes that occur on campus.

Dallas ISD Reporting of Bullying (from the Dallas ISD web page):
Reports of bullying should be made as soon as possible after the alleged act or knowledge of the alleged act. A failure to promptly report may impair the District's ability to investigate and address the prohibited conduct.

Any student who believes that he or she has experienced bullying or believes that another student has experienced bullying should immediately report the alleged acts to a teacher, counselor, principal, or other district employee. A report may be made orally or in writing.

To report after hours parents and students can contact Office of Professional Responsibility Hotline at 1-800-530-1608, which is staffed 24 hours a day.

DCCCD HELP LINES

Technical help with e-connect   972.669.6402

Or log on to: econnect.custhelp.com/app/answers/detail/a_id/396   OR   tinyurl.com/ybn4ppgb

Technical support hours are:
Monday - Friday: 7:00 a.m. – midnight; Saturday - Sunday: 3:30 p.m. – midnight

Taken from DCCCD website:
DCCCD Police
If an emergency, dial 9-1-1
Campus Police: 972-860-4290*

*According to the DCCCD web site, campus police can often respond more quickly because they are close by and know the campus.

Hearing impaired? You can text 972-860-4290 and the police will respond by text.

Distinguished Level of Achievement

Math (4 Credits)
to include Algebra 2
- ☐ MS:_____ Credits:____
- ☐ Year 1: _____ Credits:____
- ☐ Year 2: _____ Credits:____
- ☐ Year 3: _____ Credits:____
- ☐ Year 4: _____ Credits:____

Science (4 Credits)
- ☐ MS:_____ Credits:____
- ☐ Year 1: _____ Credits:____
- ☐ Year 2: _____ Credits:____
- ☐ Year 3: _____ Credits:____
- ☐ Year 4: _____ Credits:____

Language Arts (4 Credits)
- ☐ MS:_____ Credits:____
- ☐ Year 1: _____ Credits:____
- ☐ Year 2: _____ Credits:____
- ☐ Year 3: _____ Credits:____
- ☐ Year 4: _____ Credits:____

Social Studies (3 Credits)
- ☐ Year 1: _____ Credits:____
- ☐ Year 2: _____ Credits:____
- ☐ Year 3: _____ Credits:____
- ☐ _____ Credits:____

Physical Education (1 Credit)
- ☐ Year 1: _____ Credits:____
- ☐ Year 2: _____ Credits:____

Language other than English (2 Credit)
- ☐ Year 1: _____ Credits:____
- ☐ Year 2: _____ Credits:____

Electives (7 Credits)
- ☐ Year__ : _____ Credits:____
- ☐ Year__ : _____ Credits:____
- ☐ Year__ : _____ Credits:____
- ☐ Year__ : _____ Credits:____
- ☐ Year__ : _____ Credits:____
- ☐ Year__ : _____ Credits:____
- ☐ Year__ : _____ Credits:____

Fine Arts (1 Credit)
- ☐ Year__ : _____ Credits:____
- ☐ Year__ : _____ Credits:____

Total High School Credits:

Selected Endorsement Requirements (add yours here)

My College Plan

Courses that are dual credit earn BOTH high school credits and college credits. Keep track each year and take a photo of your completed course work. Ultimately, no one is more concerned about your success than you! Keeping track of these courses is part of your responsibility as a college student.

Name _____   Degree Plan: _____

TSI Scores (met or not met):   Reading _____   Writing _____   Math _____

Fall _____ ❺ (insert year)

High school course	High school course #	College Course	College Course #	Grade earned at end of semester

Spring _____ ❺ (insert year)

High school course	High school course #	College Course	College Course #	Grade earned at end of semester

What is it about reading?

According to NAEP (National Assessment of Educational Progress), only 37% of students are college ready in math and reading when they finish high school.

Reported by the College Board between 45-48% of students who enter college upon completion of high school actually have a degree after 6 years.

What do you think about that?

College & Career Ready

	Not on Track		On Track	
Grade	Falls Far Below	Approaches	Meets	Exceeds
7	625L and below	630L-965L	970L-1120L	1125L and above
8	660L and below	665L – 1005L	1010L – 1185L	1190L and above
9	775L and beow	780L – 1045L	1050L – 1250L	1255L and above
10	830L and below	835L – 1075L	1080L – 1335L	1340L and above
11/12	950L and below	955L – 1180L	1185L – 1385L	1390L and above

Data tracker: LEXILE scores

BOY	MOY	EOY

How to improve Lexile scores: READ! Read a variety of material with words that are challenging but content that is not; learn from the internet – if you don't know how to do something, *read* about it rather than watching a video.

Data tracker: TSI Reading

Last administration	Month:	Month:	Month:

Data tracker: TSI Writing

Last administration	Month:	Month:	Month:

Common Instructional Framework

Collaborative Group Work: Collaborative group work involves bringing students together in small groups for the common purpose of engaging in learning. Effective group work is well planned and strategic. Students are grouped intentionally with each student held accountable for contributing to the group work. Activities are designed so that students with diverse skill levels are supported as well as challenged by their peers. Collaborative group work uses questioning, scaffolding and classroom talk and centers literacy groups.

Classroom Talk: Classroom talk creates the space for students to articulate their thinking and strengthen their voice. Classroom talk takes place in pairs, in collaborative group work and as a whole class. As students become accustomed to talking in class, the teacher serves as a facilitator to engage students in higher levels of discourse. Classroom talk opens the space for questioning, effective scaffolding and successful collaborative group work and literacy groups.

Writing to Learn: Writing to learn is a strategy through which students can develop their ideas, their critical thinking ability and their writing skills. Writing to learn enables students to experiment every day with written language and increase their fluency and mastery of written conventions. Writing to learn can also be used as formative assessment and as a way to scaffold mid- and high-stakes writing assignments and tests.

Questioning: Questioning challenges students and teachers to use good questions as a way to open conversations and further intellectual inquiry. Effective questioning (by the teacher and by students) deepens classroom conversations and the level of discourse students apply to their work. Teachers use this strategy to create opportunities for students to investigate and analyze their thinking as well as the thinking of their peers and the authors that they read in each of their classes.

Scaffolding: Scaffolding helps students to connect prior knowledge and experience with new information. Teachers use this strategy to connect students with previous learning in a content area as well as with previous learning in an earlier grade. Scaffolding also helps facilitate thinking about a text by asking students to draw on their subjective experience and prior learning to make connections to new materials and ideas.

Literacy Groups: A specific kind of collaborative groups where students focus on text and build analysis skills. Roles are designed to divide up the thinking or processing skills in order to develop critical thinking and problem solving skills for college.

Classroom Talk Starters

If you don't agree with a group mate:
CT1 – I understand what you're saying, and I wonder if...
CT2 – I respectfully disagree because...
CT3 – I hadn't thought of it that way; my thought...

If you want to move your group along:
CT4 – Everyone has great points; let's look at what is next on the agenda.
CT5 - With respect to our time limitations, we should go to the next part.

If you are concerned about a group mate's contribution (or lack thereof):
CT6 – Let's go back to the requirements and review our individual contributions.
CT7 - I've learned that we all have many commitments outside the group, but we have to be sure to do our parts.
CT8 – Is there a way that you can get that done by _____? (specify a date and time).
CT9 – How can we eliminate the distractions? (ex: move locations, shut off cell phones)

10 generic WTLs

A – What is the most important thing I said in the last 10 minutes?
B - Explain how I can know that you know today's learning objective?
C – Write a letter a peer who is absent explaining the three most important things he missed?
D – What would happen if _____ changed?
E – How would a 7th grader struggle with this?
F – If I had to reduce this lesson by 5 minutes, what could I take out so you would still understand?
G – Give a group three things you learned today and tell why you grouped them.
H – Tell me everything you know about _____.
I – If you were <u>required</u> to reorganize today's notes in another way, explain what it would look like.
J – When thinking about what we just learned, where else have you seen something related?

Collaborative Group Work Roles

By adopting roles when asked to complete a task collaboratively, students excel because the complexity of the job is broken down. These roles typically work but it is the responsibility of the students to truly fulfill the roles. Ask your teacher for help as needed.

ROLES FOR LECTURE or VIDEO

1. **CRITIC** must identify 3 things the video or lecture could have considered to make the argument more balanced.

2. **PROPONENT** must identify 3 specific points illustrated in the video or lecture that supported the main message.

3. **SUMMARIZER** must tell what the primary message is and list supporting examples.

4. **APPLICATION PERSON** must explain one way the material in the video has a direct impact on your life.

ROLES for READINGS/ANALYSIS

1. **ILLUMINATOR** must find memorable passages or sections the group should focus extra attention on. The sections should relate to the daily objective as well as be interesting, puzzling or remind you of another learning experience.

2. **WORD MASTER** must identify words that are new, important or used in unusual ways. Remember to indicate where these words are found in the text so you can lead the discussion of the words.

3. **SUMMARIZER** must tell what the primary message is and list supporting examples.

4. **CONNECTOR** must explain how the passage connects to prior or future learning in this course, or in another course. You'll think, this reminds me of…

Multiplication table with perfect squares

	0	1	2	3	4	5	6	7	8	9	10	11	12
0	0	0	0	0	0	0	0	0	0	0	0	0	0
1	0	1	2	3	4	5	6	7	8	9	10	11	12
2	0	2	4	6	8	10	12	14	16	18	20	22	24
3	0	3	6	9	12	15	18	21	24	27	30	33	36
4	0	4	8	12	16	20	24	28	32	36	40	44	48
5	0	5	10	15	20	25	30	35	40	45	50	55	60
6	0	6	12	18	24	30	36	42	48	54	60	66	72
7	0	7	14	21	28	35	42	49	56	63	70	77	84
8	0	8	16	24	32	40	48	56	64	72	80	88	96
9	0	9	18	27	36	45	54	63	72	81	90	99	108
10	0	10	20	30	40	50	60	70	80	90	100	110	120
11	0	11	22	33	44	55	66	77	88	99	110	121	132
12	0	12	24	36	48	60	72	84	96	108	120	132	144

English rules everyone MUST know

THERE/THEIR/THEY'RE
"There" means in a place or at a place
"Their" is a possessive.
"They're" is a contraction of "they are"

They're taking their cars to the parking lot over there.

ITS/IT'S
"Its" is possessive
"It's" is a contraction of "it is"

It's common for a dog to keep its favorite toy hidden.

YOUR/YOU'RE
Your is possessive
You're is a contraction of "you are"

You're headed in the right direction with your thesis statement.

TWO/TOO/TO
Two is the number 2
Too is a synonym for also
To indicates action

Could I have two burgers to go, too?

WHOSE/WHO'S
Whose is possessive
Who's is a contraction of "who is"

Who's the person whose bike is parked outside?

LOSE/LOOSE
Lose is to not win.
Loose is the opposite of tight (fitting)

Did you lose that loose fitting jacket?

Costa's Level of Inquiry

Level One Questions (Text Explicit) Readers can point to one correct answer right in the text. Words found in these questions include: • defining • observing • describing • naming • identifying • reciting • noting • listing	**Level 1 statement** • Define irony. (English) • Identify the starting date of the American Revolution. (History) • Define tangent. (Math) • Define photosynthesis. (Science)
Level Two Questions (Text Implicit) Readers infer answers from what the text implicitly states, finding answers in several places in the text. Words found in these questions include: • analyzing • grouping • synthesizing • comparing/contrasting • inferring • sequencing	**Level 2 Statement** • Compare and contrast Mr. Frank and Mr. Van Daan in Anne Frank: Diary of a Young Girl. (English) • Analyze the causes of the American Revolution. (History) • Compare the square root of 49 to the square root of 64. Which is greater? (Math) • Diagram and order the stages of photosynthesis. (Science)
Level Three Questions (Experience Based) Readers think beyond what the text states. Answers are based on reader's prior knowledge/experience and will vary. Words found in these questions include: • evaluating • judging • applying a principle • speculating • imagining • predicting • hypothesizing	**Level 3 Statement** • Predict how Charlie Gordon will change after his operation in Flowers for Algernon. (English) • Imagine you were a soldier fighting in the Civil War. How would you feel? (History) • Apply the Pythagorean theorem to the find the measurement of this triangle. (Math) • Diagram the stages of photosynthesis and predict how long each takes. (Science)

Month:		
Sunday	Monday	Tuesday

	Wednesday	Thursday	Friday	Saturday

Week of

Monday	Tuesday

Wednesday	Thursday

Friday	Saturday/Sunday

This week's reflection

Week of

Monday	Tuesday

Wednesday	Thursday

Friday	Saturday/Sunday

This week's reflection

Week of

Monday	Tuesday

Wednesday	Thursday

Friday	Saturday/Sunday

This week's reflection

Week of

Monday	Tuesday

Wednesday	Thursday

Friday	Saturday/Sunday

This week's reflection

Week of

Monday

Tuesday

Wednesday

Thursday

Friday

Saturday/Sunday

This week's reflection

additional notes

Month:		
Sunday	Monday	Tuesday

Wednesday	Thursday	Friday	Saturday

Week of

Monday	Tuesday

Wednesday	Thursday

Friday	Saturday/Sunday

This week's reflection

Week of

Monday	Tuesday

Wednesday	Thursday

Friday	Saturday/Sunday

This week's reflection

Week of

Monday	Tuesday

Wednesday	Thursday

Friday	Saturday/Sunday

This week's reflection

Week of

Monday	Tuesday

Wednesday	Thursday

Friday	Saturday/Sunday

This week's reflection

Week of

Monday	Tuesday

Wednesday	Thursday

Friday	Saturday/Sunday

This week's reflection

additional notes

Month:		
Sunday	Monday	Tuesday

Wednesday	Thursday	Friday	Saturday

Week of

Monday	Tuesday

Wednesday	Thursday

Friday	Saturday/Sunday

This week's reflection

Week of

Monday	Tuesday

Wednesday	Thursday

Friday	Saturday/Sunday

This week's reflection

Week of

Monday	Tuesday

Wednesday	Thursday

Friday	Saturday/Sunday

This week's reflection

Week of

Monday	Tuesday

Wednesday	Thursday

Friday	Saturday/Sunday

This week's reflection

Week of

Monday	Tuesday

Wednesday	Thursday

Friday	Saturday/Sunday

This week's reflection

additional notes

Month:		
Sunday	Monday	Tuesday

Wednesday	Thursday	Friday	Saturday

Week of

Monday

Tuesday

Wednesday

Thursday

Friday

Saturday/Sunday

This week's reflection

Week of

Monday	Tuesday

Wednesday	Thursday

Friday	Saturday/Sunday

This week's reflection

Week of

Monday	Tuesday

Wednesday	Thursday

Friday	Saturday/Sunday

This week's reflection

Week of

Monday	Tuesday

Wednesday	Thursday

Friday	Saturday/Sunday

This week's reflection

Week of

Monday	Tuesday

Wednesday	Thursday

Friday	Saturday/Sunday

This week's reflection

additional notes

Month:		
Sunday	Monday	Tuesday

Wednesday	Thursday	Friday	Saturday

Week of

Monday	Tuesday

Wednesday	Thursday

Friday	Saturday/Sunday

This week's reflection

Week of

Monday	Tuesday

Wednesday	Thursday

Friday	Saturday/Sunday

This week's reflection

Week of

Monday	Tuesday

Wednesday	Thursday

Friday	Saturday/Sunday

This week's reflection

Week of

Monday	Tuesday

Wednesday	Thursday

Friday	Saturday/Sunday

This week's reflection

Week of

Monday	Tuesday

Wednesday	Thursday

Friday	Saturday/Sunday

This week's reflection

additional notes

Month:		
Sunday	Monday	Tuesday

	Wednesday	Thursday	Friday	Saturday

Week of

Monday	Tuesday

Wednesday	Thursday

Friday	Saturday/Sunday

This week's reflection

Week of

Monday	Tuesday

Wednesday	Thursday

Friday	Saturday/Sunday

This week's reflection

Week of

Monday	Tuesday

Wednesday	Thursday

Friday	Saturday/Sunday

This week's reflection

Week of

Monday	Tuesday

Wednesday	Thursday

Friday	Saturday/Sunday

This week's reflection

Week of

Monday

Tuesday

Wednesday

Thursday

Friday

Saturday/Sunday

This week's reflection

additional notes

Month:		
Sunday	Monday	Tuesday

Wednesday	Thursday	Friday	Saturday

Week of

Monday

Tuesday

Wednesday

Thursday

Friday

Saturday/Sunday

This week's reflection

Week of

Monday	Tuesday

Wednesday	Thursday

Friday	Saturday/Sunday

This week's reflection

Week of

Monday

Tuesday

Wednesday

Thursday

Friday

Saturday/Sunday

This week's reflection

Week of

Monday	Tuesday

Wednesday	Thursday

Friday	Saturday/Sunday

This week's reflection

Week of

Monday

Tuesday

Wednesday

Thursday

Friday

Saturday/Sunday

This week's reflection

additional notes

Month:

Sunday	Monday	Tuesday

Wednesday	Thursday	Friday	Saturday

Week of

Monday	Tuesday

Wednesday	Thursday

Friday	Saturday/Sunday

This week's reflection

Week of

Monday	Tuesday

Wednesday	Thursday

Friday	Saturday/Sunday

This week's reflection

Week of

Monday	Tuesday

Wednesday	Thursday

Friday	Saturday/Sunday

This week's reflection

Week of

Monday	Tuesday

Wednesday	Thursday

Friday	Saturday/Sunday

This week's reflection

Week of

Monday	Tuesday
Wednesday	Thursday
Friday	Saturday/Sunday

This week's reflection

additional notes

Month:

Sunday	Monday	Tuesday

Wednesday	Thursday	Friday	Saturday

Week of

Monday	Tuesday

Wednesday	Thursday

Friday	Saturday/Sunday

This week's reflection

Week of

Monday	Tuesday

Wednesday	Thursday

Friday	Saturday/Sunday

This week's reflection

Week of

Monday	Tuesday

Wednesday	Thursday

Friday	Saturday/Sunday

This week's reflection

Week of

Monday	Tuesday

Wednesday	Thursday

Friday	Saturday/Sunday

This week's reflection

Week of

Monday	Tuesday

Wednesday	Thursday

Friday	Saturday/Sunday

This week's reflection

additional notes

Month:		
Sunday	Monday	Tuesday

Wednesday	Thursday	Friday	Saturday

Week of

Monday	Tuesday

Wednesday	Thursday

Friday	Saturday/Sunday

This week's reflection

Week of

Monday	Tuesday

Wednesday	Thursday

Friday	Saturday/Sunday

This week's reflection

Week of

Monday	Tuesday

Wednesday	Thursday

Friday	Saturday/Sunday

This week's reflection

Week of

Monday	Tuesday

Wednesday	Thursday

Friday	Saturday/Sunday

This week's reflection

Week of

Monday	Tuesday

Wednesday	Thursday

Friday	Saturday/Sunday

This week's reflection

additional notes

Month:		
Sunday	Monday	Tuesday

	Wednesday	Thursday	Friday	Saturday

Week of

Monday	Tuesday
Wednesday	Thursday
Friday	Saturday/Sunday

This week's reflection

Week of

Monday	Tuesday

Wednesday	Thursday

Friday	Saturday/Sunday

This week's reflection

Week of

Monday

Tuesday

Wednesday

Thursday

Friday

Saturday/Sunday

This week's reflection

Week of

Monday	Tuesday

Wednesday	Thursday

Friday	Saturday/Sunday

This week's reflection

Week of

Monday	Tuesday

Wednesday	Thursday

Friday	Saturday/Sunday

This week's reflection

additional notes

Month:		
Sunday	Monday	Tuesday

Wednesday	Thursday	Friday	Saturday

Week of

Monday	Tuesday

Wednesday	Thursday

Friday	Saturday/Sunday

This week's reflection

Week of

Monday	Tuesday

Wednesday	Thursday

Friday	Saturday/Sunday

This week's reflection

Week of

Monday	Tuesday
Wednesday	Thursday
Friday	Saturday/Sunday

This week's reflection

Week of

Monday	Tuesday

Wednesday	Thursday

Friday	Saturday/Sunday

This week's reflection

Week of

Monday	Tuesday

Wednesday	Thursday

Friday	Saturday/Sunday

This week's reflection

ATLAS

Africa

Reading Tracker - Pages in a Week

wk 1	wk 2	wk 3	wk 4	wk 5	wk 6	wk 7	wk 8	wk 9	wk 10	wk 11	wk 12	wk 13	wk 14	wk 15

Reading Tracker - Pages in a Week

wk 1	wk 2	wk 3	wk 4	wk 5	wk 6	wk 7	wk 8	wk 9	wk 10	wk 11	wk 12	wk 13	wk 14	wk 15

Self Tracker - Unit Tests

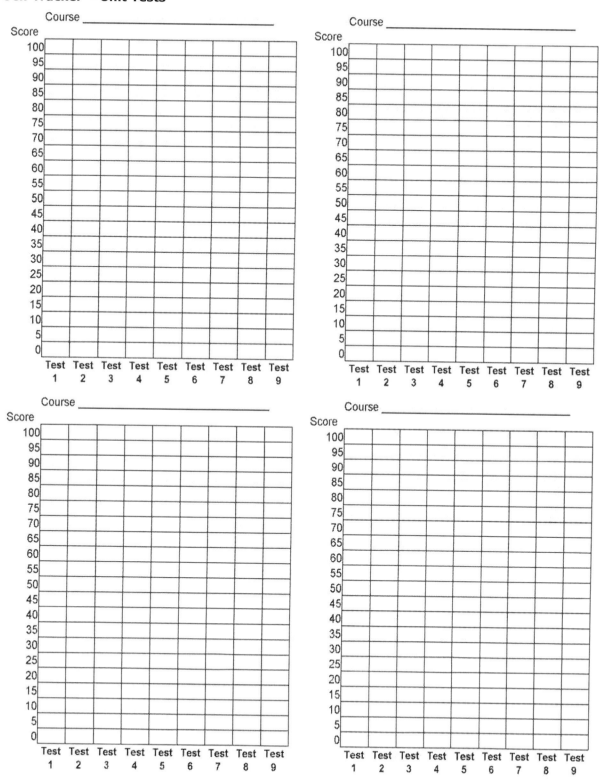

Self Tracker - Unit Tests

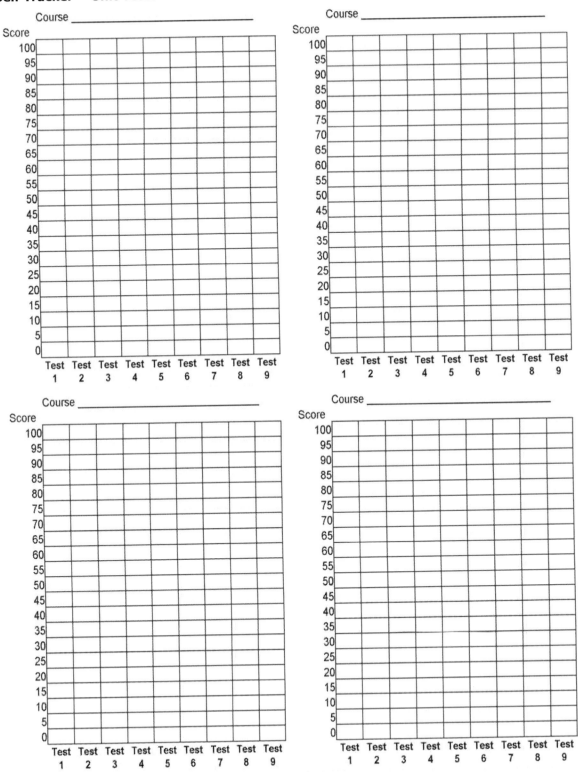

GMETRIX TRACKER

MOS Program	Module	Date Completed	Score	P/F	Mode	Retake	Date
Power-point	Practice Exam 1 Training	8/20/18	90%	Pass	Training	No	
Word	Core Practice Exam 1 Training	8/22/18	60%	Fail	Testing	Yes	8/23

MOS Program	Module	Date Completed	Score	P/F	Mode	Retake	Date

Classroom Lessons with Microsoft Programs

Program	Class	Brief Description	Date
Ex: Power Point	*Biology*	*Made 4 slides to explain parts of cell*	*9-22*

Dual Credit Program Monitoring - *Please include the name of your college courses and earned grade or points earned (for example 75% or 300/400 points)*

Semester _____   Year _____

College course Date →	Ck point 1	Ck point 2	Ck point 3	Ck point 4	Ck point 5	Ck point 6	Ck point 7
1.							
2.							
3.							
4.							
Student initials							
Counselor's initials							

Semester _____   Year _____

College course Date →	Ck point 1	Ck point 2	Ck point 3	Ck point 4	Ck point 5	Ck point 6	Ck point 7
1.							
2.							
3.							
4.							
Student initials							
Counselor's initials							

Missing Assignments Tracker

Date	Course	Missing Assignment	Reason	Parent Signature

Determine what you need to complete assignments. Include which staff member will be your accountability partner. Keeping up with assignments is a characteristic of college-ready students.

Missing Assignments Tracker

Date	Course	Missing Assignment	Reason	Parent Signature

Determine what you need to complete assignments. Include which staff member will be your accountability partner. Keeping up with assignments is a characteristic of college-ready students.

Missing Assignments Tracker

Date	Course	Missing Assignment	Reason	Parent Signature

Determine what you need to complete assignments. Include which staff member will be your accountability partner. Keeping up with assignments is a characteristic of college-ready students.

Math Formulas

polynomials

Perfect Square Trinomials:	$a^2 + 2ab + b^2 = (a+b)^2 \qquad a^2 - 2ab + b^2 = (a-b)^2$
Difference of Squares:	$a^2 - b^2 = (a-b)(a+b)$
Sum of Cubes:	$a^3 + b^3 = (a+b)(a^2 - ab + b^2)$
Difference of Cubes:	$a^3 - b^3 = (a-b)(a^2 + ab + b^2)$
Square of a Sum:	$(a+b)^2 = (a+b)(a+b) = a^2 + 2ab + b^2$
Square of a Difference:	$(a-b)^2 = (a-b)(a-b) = a^2 - 2ab + b^2$
Product of a Sum and a Difference:	$(a+b)(a-b) = a^2 - b^2$

logarithms

Product Property:	$\log_x ab = \log_x a + \log_x b$
Quotient Property:	$\log_x \dfrac{a}{b} = \log_x a - \log_x b,\ b \neq 0$
Power Property:	$\log_b m^p = p \log_b m$
Change of Base:	$\log_a n = \dfrac{\log_b n}{\log_b a}$

Midpoint:	$M = \left(\dfrac{x_1 + x_2}{2},\ \dfrac{y_1 + y_2}{2} \right)$
Distance:	$d = \sqrt{(x_2 - x_1)^2 + (y_2 - y_1)^2}$
Slope:	$m = \dfrac{y_2 - y_1}{x_2 - x_1}$

quadratics

Vertex Form:	$f(x) = a(x-h)^2 + k$
Parabolas:	$(x-h)^2 = 4py(y-k)$ $(y-k)^2 = 4py(x-h)$

exponents

Product of powers	$a^m a^n = a^{(m+n)}$
Quotient of powers	$\dfrac{a^m}{a^n} = a^{(m-n)}$
Power of a power	$(a^m)^n = a^{mn}$
Rational exponent	$a^{\frac{m}{n}} = \sqrt[n]{a^m}$
Negative exponent	$a^{-n} = \dfrac{1}{a^n}$

factoring

Perfect square trinomials	$a^2 + 2ab + b^2 = (a+b)^2$ $a^2 - 2ab + b^2 = (a-b)^2$
Difference of squares	$a^2 - b^2 = (a-b)(a+b)$

linear

Standard form	$Ax + By = C$
Slope-intercept form	$y = mx + b$
Point-slope form	$y - y_1 = m(x - x_1)$
Slope of a line	$m = \dfrac{y_2 - y_1}{x_2 - x_1}$

quadratic

Standard form	$f(x) = ax^2 + bx + c$
Vertex form	$f(x) = a(x-h)^2 + k$
Quadratic formula	$x = \dfrac{-b \pm \sqrt{b^2 - 4ac}}{2a}$
Axis of symmetry	$x = \dfrac{-b}{2a}$

Rules for Transformation

Transformation	Function	Description
Horizontal shift	$f(x + h)$	Shift left **h** units
	$f(x - h)$	Shift right **h** units
Vertical shift	$f(x) + k$	Shift up **k** units
	$f(x) - k$	Shift down **k** units
Reflection	$-f(x)$	Reflect across **x**-axis
	$f(-x)$	Reflect across **y**-axis
Vertical stretch/ compress	$af(x)$ where $a > 1$	Stretch vertically by factor of a
	$af(x)$ $0 < a < 1$	Stretch vertically by factor of a
Horizontal stretch/ compress	$F(ax)$ $a > 1$	Stretch horizontally by factor of $\frac{1}{a}$
	$F(ax)$ $0 < a < 1$	Stretch horizontally by factor of $\frac{1}{a}$

Linear function

Domain: All real numbers
Range: All real numbers

Vertical line - Undefined - $-x = \#$ (ex: x = 4)

Horizontal line - zero slope - $y = \#$ (ex: y=-2)

Parallel: the slope (m) is same.
Perpendicular: the slope(m) is opposite and reciprocal

Standard form $ax + by = c$

Slope-Int form $f(x) = mx + b$
　　m: slope　　b: y-intercept

Quadratic Function

$f(x) = ax^2 + bx + c$
　　Parabola which is U-shaped.
c: y-intercept

Domain: all real number
Range:
{y ≥ minimum value} when a is positive
{y ≥ maximum value} when a is negative

Logarithmic Function

$f(x) = \log_b x$
b: base (b ≠ 0, b > 0)
Domain: x>0
Range: all real numbers
Vertical asymptote: x=0
x-intercept: (1, 0)
Y-intercept: none

Exponential Function

$f(x) = ab^x$
a: initial value
b: growth/decay factor

Domain: all real number
Range: y>0

Horizontal asymptote: y=0
Y-intercept: (0, a)
x- intercept: none

PLANNER CHECK

Planner check grades are EASY grades. Steps I have to complete to earn 100%:
-
-
-
-

First six weeks	1	2	3	
	4	5	6	
Second six weeks	1	2	3	
	4	5	6	
Third six weeks	1	2	3	
	4	5	6	

Why do I use a planner?
- *Due dates are easy to find*
- *Easy to find time for leisure activities*
- *Life-long routine that I need…because life just keeps getting busier*
-
-

	1	2	3	
Fourth six weeks				
	4	5	6	
Fifth six weeks	1	2	3	
	4	5	6	
Sixth six weeks	1	2	3	
	4	5	6	

2019-20 Dallas ISD /DCCCD Combined Calendar

AUG

S	M	T	W	TH	F	S
				1	2	3
4	5	6	7	8	9	10
11	12	13	14	15	16	17
18	[19	20	21	22	23	24
25	(26)	27	28	29	30	31

19: 1st day ISD   26: 1st day IHE

SEPT

S	M	T	W	TH	F	S
1	2	3	4	5	6	7
8	9	10	11	12	13	14
15	16	17	18	19	20	21
22	23	24	25	26	27]	28
29	[30					

2: holiday ISD   2: holiday IHE

OCT

S	M	T	W	TH	F	S
		1	2	3	4	5
6	7	8	9	10	11	12
13	14	15	16	17	18	19
20	21	22	23	24	25	26
27	28	29	30	31		

18: holiday ISD

NOV

S	M	T	W	TH	F	S
					1]	2
3	[4	5	6	7	8	9
10	11	12	13	14	15	16
17	18	19	20	21	22	23
24	25	26	27	28	29	30

25—29— holiday ISD   28,29—holiday IHE

DEC

S	M	T	W	TH	F	S
1	2	3	4	5	6	7
8	9	10	11	(12)	13	14
15	16	17	18	19]	20	21
22	23	24	25	26	27	28
29	30	31				

20—31: holiday ISD   12: semester ends IHE

JAN

S	M	T	W	TH	F	S
			1	2	3	4
5	6	7	[8	9	10	11
12	13	14	15	16	17	18
19	20	(21)	22	23	24	25
26	27	28	29	30	31	

1—7, 20: holiday ISD   21: first day IHE

FEB

S	M	T	W	TH	F	S
						1
2	3	4	5	6	7	8
9	10	11	12	13	14	15
16	17	18	19	20	21]	22
23	[24	25	26	27	28	29

14, 17: holiday ISD   27, 28: holiday IHE

MAR

S	M	T	W	TH	F	S
1	2	3	4	5	6	7
8	9	10	11	12	13	14
15	16	17	18	19	20	21
22	23	24	25	26	27	28
29	30	31				

16-20: Spring Break

APR

S	M	T	W	TH	F	S
			1	2	3	4
5	6	7	8	9]	10	11
12	[13	14	15	16	17	18
19	20	21	22	23	24	25
26	27	28	29	30		

10: Holiday for both   13: inclement weather ISD

MAY

S	M	T	W	TH	F	S
					1	2
3	4	5	6	7	8	9
10	11	12	13	(14)	15	16
17	18	19	20	21	22	23
24/31	25	26	27]	28	29	30

25: holiday ISD   14: semester ends IHE
27: semester ends
1: inclement weather

JUNE

S	M	T	W	TH	F	S
	1	2	3	4	5	6
7	8	9	10	11	12	13
14	15	16	17	18	19	20
21	22	23	24	25	26	27
28	29	30				

My dates to remember:

Made in the
USA
Lexington, KY